SHARKS

GET UP CLOSE TO THE OCEANS' **MOST FEARED HUNTERS**

Bath · New York · Cologne · Melbourne · Delhi
Hong Kong · Shenzhen · Singapore · Amsterdam

This edition published by Parragon Books Ltd
in 2015 and distributed by

Parragon Inc.
440 Park Avenue South, 13th Floor
New York, NY 10016
www.parragon.com

This edition © Parragon Books Ltd 2013–2015

This edition produced by Jollands Editions
Cover design by JC Lanaway

Original edition designed, produced, and
packaged by Stonecastle Graphics Ltd

©2015 Discovery Communications, LLC.
Discovery Kids and the
Discovery Kids logo are trademarks of
Discovery Communications, LLC, used under
license. All rights reserved. discoverykids.com

ISBN 978-1-4723-7676-3

Printed in China

Cover images courtesy of istock

CONTENTS

INTRODUCTION

Sharks are found in all the oceans of the world.
Some are fierce meat-eaters that rip their prey
to shreds; others feed on tiny plants and animals,
called plankton, that drift along in the ocean currents.

Our planet was formed around 4.5 billion years
ago. The first living creatures appeared roughly
1.2 billion years later. Life in the oceans evolved
slowly, until sharks appeared around 400 million
years ago. Since then, sharks have evolved into
over 470 different species. Zoologists group
these into families, and classify the families in
larger groups called "orders," to show how they
are related to each other.

The longest existing modern sharks are the
cow sharks (sixgill and sevengill), which date
back 190 million years. These primitive species
can be found in the deep sea. The newest
modern sharks are the hammerheads, which
are thought to date back 50 million years.
Sharks are among the oldest creatures to have
been living continuously on Earth.

The term *shark* was first used in 1569 to
advertise a specimen that was brought back
to London, England, and exhibited there.
Sailors had caught it during an expedition to
South America commanded by the famous
Elizabethan seaman Captain John Hawkins.
Why they called it a "shark" remains a mystery.

Sharks live in various marine habitats around
the world. Most prefer temperate and tropical
waters, but some are found in colder seas near
the North and South Poles. They range from
the shallow waters near the coastline right out
to the open ocean, and some even live in deep
waters where light does not reach.

DIFFERENT TYPES OF SHARK

Some sharks are tiny, others are giants. Some are gentle, and some are fierce. Some swim very fast to catch their prey in the open sea. Others move slowly and feed on animals that live on the ocean floor.

Fin
Stiff fins are supported by rods of cartilage.

Gills
Gills are used to breathe.

Snout
The snout is often sharply pointed. The mouth is shaped like a crescent.

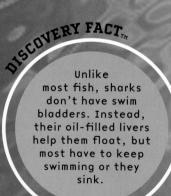

DISCOVERY FACT™

Unlike most fish, sharks don't have swim bladders. Instead, their oil-filled livers help them float, but most have to keep swimming or they sink.

Dogfish have long, slim bodies to slip through the water.

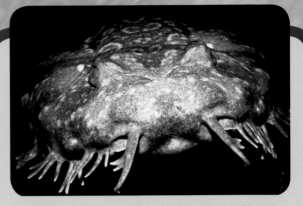

Wobbegongs hide on the seabed. They are well camouflaged.

Tail
A strong pointed tail fin pushes the shark through the water.

Angel sharks have flat bodies. They also hide on the seabed.

Basking sharks live in open water. They are often seen swimming very close to the coastline.

AMAZING SHARKS

Can you imagine a fish that has a head shaped like a hammer? Or one that can gobble up a sea lion whole? Sharks are some of the world's most amazing creatures.

Great white shark

The great white shark eats other sharks for dinner—along with whole penguins, seals, and sea lions.

Whale shark

The gentle whale shark is the world's biggest fish. It weighs as much as two elephants and can grow longer than a bus.

Mako shark

The bullet-shaped mako shark can swim at over 43 miles per hour (69 km/h). It is one of the fastest fish in the ocean.

Hammerhead shark

The hammerhead shark has eyes on the sides of its distinctively shaped head. By swinging its head from side to side it can get an all-around view.

DISCOVERY FACT™

Sharks don't have bones. Their skeletons are made of light, stretchy cartilage, like the material in human ears and noses.

Hammerhead sharks have smaller pectoral fins than other species of shark.

HOW SHARKS SWIM

Most sharks are graceful and powerful swimmers. Their smooth bodies are perfect for moving underwater. Sharks swim in S-shaped movements, powered by their tails.

Dorsal fin
The stiff fin on a shark's back helps with balance.

Tail
The shark's tail is a little bit like its motor. It sweeps it from side to side in long strokes, powering its body forward. The streamlined shape of the shark's body helps it glide through the water. Sharks with large tails can accelerate very quickly.

Pectoral fins
Fins on each side of a shark's body help it steer.

Fins
The dorsal fin on the shark's back acts like the keel of a boat. It stops the shark from rolling over in the water. The pectoral fins on the sides help to move the shark up and down in the water, like the wings of an aircraft.

DISCOVERY FACT™
Sharks cannot swim backward. This is because their stiff pectoral fins will not bend upward like those of other fish, so they can't back up.

Tail

A shark's long tail beats from side to side, pushing the shark forward through the water.

Types of tail

The caudal, or tail, fins of sharks vary a lot in shape and size. The top half of the fin is usually larger than the bottom half because the shark's backbone extends into the upper half of the fin.

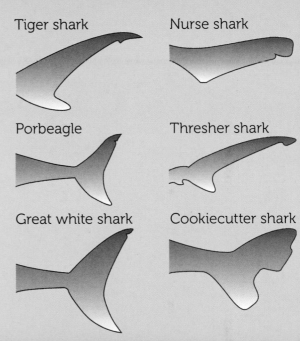

Tiger shark

Nurse shark

Porbeagle

Thresher shark

Great white shark

Cookiecutter shark

Slow motion

Whale sharks are slow swimmers, cruising along at about 3 miles per hour (5 km/h). They swim by moving their entire bodies from side to side, not just their tails.

SENSES AND HUNTING

Sharks are always seeking out their next meal. They can see, hear, touch, and smell, just like people. But their senses are much more powerful than ours and are perfectly adapted to working in water.

Touch

Finding food

A shark uses all its senses to find prey, but smell gives it some of the most important clues. A shark can smell a tiny amount of blood in the water from hundreds of feet away.

Touch

A lateral line along their sides helps sharks pick up movements in the water around them.

Hearing

A shark's ears can hear sounds traveling through the water. The ears lie beneath small holes in the shark's head.

Extra sense

Sharks have special jelly-filled receptors in their heads. These extra sense organs pick up the faint electric signals given off by other fish. This sense is particularly powerful in hammerhead sharks.

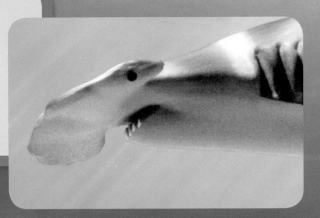

Sight

Hearing

Smell

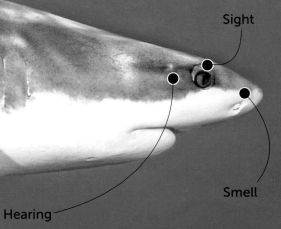

Sight

A shark's eyes can see well in dim underwater light.

Smell

A shark does not breathe through its nose. It is just used for detecting smell.

TEETH

Teeth are a shark's most important weapon. They are designed to help it catch and eat prey.

Sharks have multiple rows of teeth. Every time a shark loses a tooth, the tooth in the row behind it moves forward to take the lost tooth's place.

The shape of a shark's tooth depends on its diet. Sharks that eat fish have long, narrow teeth for gripping slippery fish. Sharks that eat mammals, such as seal, have sharp, jagged teeth for ripping flesh. Sharks that eat shellfish have thick, platelike teeth to crush the shells of their prey.

Sharks' teeth are not rooted in the jaw like ours, but are attached to the skin covering the jaw.

Unlike in most animals, the shark's upper jaw is not rigidly attached to its skull, but hinged, so it can move its whole mouth forward and open it very wide to bite its prey.

The great white shark has sharp, pointed teeth, perfect for ripping flesh.

DISCOVERY FACT™

The great white shark has around 300 teeth at any one time, arranged in up to seven rows, but will grow many thousands of teeth over its lifetime.

The prehistoric shark megalodon may have been up to 65 feet (20 m) long. Here is one of its huge teeth next to the tooth of a modern shark (right).

The powerful tail of a great white shark helps propel it through the water, to attack prey.

The small cookiecutter shark swims up to a larger fish, takes a bite out of its side (the shape of a cookie), and swims away again very quickly!

MOTHERS AND PUPS

All baby sharks are born from eggs and are known as pups. The eggs of most sharks grow inside their mother. A few kinds of shark lay their eggs on the seabed, safe inside tough egg cases.

All sharks are born from eggs that are fertilized by sperm from the male shark. But the eggs can grow in different ways. In some sharks, they remain inside the mother's body and hatch inside her. The young shark pups are then born as live fish, ready to swim away.

Other sharks lay their eggs inside tough, leathery egg cases in the water. The pup grows inside the egg case, feeding on the yolk inside it. When it is ready to be born, the young shark wriggles its way out of the case, which splits open.

Little hammerheads
Baby hammerhead sharks are born with their heads bent backward, so they don't get stuck inside their mother.

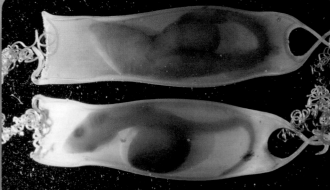

Egg cases
Dogfish eggs are protected by an egg case called a "mermaid's purse." The babies grow inside, feeding on the egg yolk.

A blue shark mother can give birth to 50 or more young at a time—the record is 135 pups. They take 9 to 12 months to grow big enough to be born.

Groups of sharks

Sharks do not remain in a family group. When sharks are seen together in a large group, it is usually because a lot of food is available to be eaten.

Lemon sharks

Lemon shark eggs grow inside their mother. She gives birth to tiny pups, which soon swim off to find food. They remain in fairly shallow water while they grow to their adult size of almost 7 feet (2 m) long. This can take between 12 and 15 years.

COASTAL NURSERIES

Many animals visit coastal waters to breed or to have their young. These shallow waters are often sheltered, and there is plenty of food for the young animals.

Hammerhead gathering

Each year, hammerhead sharks gather together in special breeding places. Each male selects a female, and they then mate. After about ten months, the female swims into shallow water to give birth to her pups.

Hammerhead sharks gather to breed.

DISCOVERY FACT™

Female lemon sharks return to the same place every two years to give birth, but males rove about, ensuring genetic diversity in the species.

Whale migration

Many whales make regular journeys along the coasts. Humpback whales spend the summer in cold waters, where there is plenty of food, then migrate to warmer waters, where they give birth to their young. Great white and tiger sharks may prey on the calves.

Underwater flier

Manta rays live in the deep sea but give birth in shallow coastal waters, where the young stay for several years. The females are pregnant for about a year before giving birth to one or two pups.

FOOD CHAINS

A food chain shows how nutrients pass from plants to animals as one eats the other. In the ocean, plant plankton is eaten by animal plankton, or zooplankton. The zooplankton is eaten by larger animals. These animals are then eaten by even bigger animals. Many sharks have a diet of seals, turtles, fish, and even large seabirds. Some sharks, however, such as the whale shark and basking shark, eat plankton and small fish.

Plant plankton

Plant plankton are at the bottom of the ocean food chains. They are called producers because they make their own food using sunlight.

Top meat-eaters

Top carnivores, or meat-eaters, such as pelicans, sharks, and dolphins, eat fish. A top carnivore is an animal that no other animal eats—they are at the top of the ocean food chain.

Plant-eaters

Zooplankton, or plant-eaters, such as this crab larva, eat the producers, or plant plankton. The plant-eaters are known as primary consumers.

Meat-eaters

Larger animals, called the secondary consumers, eat the primary consumers. Secondary consumers are hunters. There are many different hunters in the ocean, including fish and squid.

This great white shark has leaped out of the water to catch a seal.

The darker shade of this shark's back blends with the sea, so that it can attack prey from below.

DISCOVERY FACT™

The great white shark attacks its prey from underneath: it swims until it is a few yards below, then turns its head up and surges up through the water.

PLANKTON FEEDERS

Animal and plant plankton are the favorite food of many animals, including ocean giants such as the whale shark and basking shark. Most plankton feeders filter, or sieve, tiny organisms from the water.

Basking shark

The basking shark swims along with its mouth wide open. When its mouth is full of water, the fish closes it and squeezes the water out through its gill slits. Any food is trapped inside by rakers (bristlelike filters) in the gills.

Manta ray

Most rays live on the seabed, hunting fish and small animals. The huge manta ray is different. It is an active fish that swims great distances, filtering plankton through its gills.

Scientists believe that some whale sharks may live for as long as 180 years. The males are not ready to breed until they are around 30 years old.

Humpback whales have frilly plates in their mouths that sieve the water.

Whale shark

The whale shark is the largest fish in the world. It can grow up to 40 feet (12 m) long and weigh more than 23 tons (21,000 kg). It is a filter feeder, and despite its size, it is not a dangerous shark to humans.

A whale shark's spots are unique and can be used to identify an individual shark, like a human fingerprint.

BASKING SHARK

This incredible-looking shark is the second largest fish (after the whale shark) in the oceans. It may look frightening, but this is a gentle giant. It feeds on tiny plankton as it cruises slowly near the surface.

The body of the basking shark is grayish brown to dark gray, sometimes with lighter patches on the flanks. Its head is quite pointed, but as soon as the shark starts to feed, its appearance changes dramatically. Its huge jaws gape open to allow water to pour over the gill rakers inside its throat. These trap the tiny particles of plankton on which it feeds. This is called filter feeding. Nearly 400,000 gallons (about 1.5 million liters) of water pass over its bristly gill rakers every hour.

Basking sharks feed near the surface, where the tiny plankton organisms are attracted to the sunlight. Fishermen see them fairly often off the coastline. Basking sharks migrate thousands of miles during the winter months, seeking clouds of plankton (called "blooms") in warmer waters.

Mouth
A huge mouth like an enormous butterfly net sweeps up tiny food organisms in the water.

Large gill slits
Bristles behind the gill slits, called "gill rakers," trap food particles in the water.

Basking sharks are believed to take 12–20 years to reach maturity, and to have a life expectancy of about 50 years.

Profile

Length:	Up to 30 ft/9 m (males), 33 ft/10 m (females)
Weight:	Up to 8,000 lb (3,600 kg)
Order:	Mackerel sharks
Family:	Basking sharks
Diet:	Phytoplankton, zooplankton, tiny fish, fish eggs

Location

The basking shark is found in temperate (50–64°F/10–18°C) and subpolar (below 50°F/10°C) waters of the North and South Atlantic and Pacific Oceans. They swim from the ocean surface to about 1,870 feet (570 m) deep.

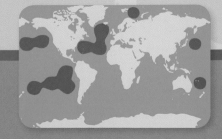

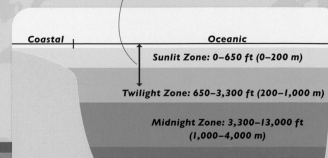

Coastal | Oceanic

Sunlit Zone: 0–650 ft (0–200 m)

Twilight Zone: 650–3,300 ft (200–1,000 m)

Midnight Zone: 3,300–13,000 ft (1,000–4,000 m)

Lower Midnight Zone: 13,000–20,000 ft (4,000–6,000 m)

LEOPARD SHARK

Leopard sharks are one of the most common sharks along the coast of California. They live in the shallow waters of bays and estuaries, and they occasionally patrol the kelp forest, usually staying near the bottom.

This handsomely marked shark has silvery-bronze skin that is covered with darker oval spots. These markings are what give it its name. The older a leopard shark is, the paler the spots will be.

Large schools of leopard sharks are a common sight in bays and estuaries. They swim over sandy or muddy flats or rock-strewn areas near kelp beds and reefs. Leopard sharks often follow the tide onto shallow-sloped shorelines to forage for food on the seabed.

Leopard sharks capture their prey by sucking water in with their mouths. This sucks up the food, which is then gripped by the teeth.

Leopard sharks are a target for fishermen, who catch them to sell as food. Live leopard sharks are also sold for keeping in aquariums.

DISCOVERY FACT™

Leopard sharks are ovoviviparous: 30 or more young hatch inside the mother, and are born alive in warm, very shallow waters in summer.

Skin
The silvery-bronze skin is patterned with dark ovals that stretch in a neat row across the back.

Profile

Length:	28–47 in/0.7–1.2 m (males), 43–59 in/1.1–1.5 m (females)
Weight:	Up to 41 lb (18.4 kg)
Order:	Ground sharks
Family:	Hound sharks
Diet:	Bony fish, crabs, clams, shrimps (right), worms

Mouth
The mouth is on the flat underside of its head, and it opens downward. This is perfect for a shark that skims over the sand to pluck up crabs, clams, and worms.

Location
The leopard shark is found in shallow temperate (50–64°F/10–18°C) water along the Pacific coast of North America. They swim from the shallows to about 300 feet (90 m) deep.

Coastal | Oceanic

Sunlit Zone: 0–650 ft (0–200 m)

Twilight Zone: 650–3,300 ft (200–1,000 m)

Midnight Zone: 3,300–13,000 ft (1,000–4,000 m)

Lower Midnight Zone: 13,000–20,000 ft (4,000–6,000 m)

NURSE SHARK

The nurse shark is one of the more docile types of shark. It is fairly lazy during the day, resting in groups on the bottom of the sea. It starts moving at night, which is when it hunts for food.

Nurse sharks are yellowish tan to dark brown in color. Young sharks sometimes have small black spots and bands on their skin.

They like warm water and live near the bottom in the shallows, sometimes close to mud or sand flats.

Unlike some sharks, nurse sharks can breathe without having to move through the water. Their respiratory system pumps water over the gills while they rest during the day.

Nurse sharks are bottom feeders. They use their sensitive barbels to search for food in the sand and silt on the ocean floor. They suck up food like a vacuum cleaner, rather than having to grasp it with their teeth.

Barbels
Thin, whiskerlike organs on the lower jaw, called "barbels," help the shark to find food in the sand and mud of the seafloor.

DISCOVERY FACT™

Nurse sharks don't get their name from being specially good mothers—it probably comes from *hurse*, an Old English word for a seafloor shark.

Profile

Length:	Average 6.9 ft/2.1 m (males), 7.9 ft/2.4 m (females)
Weight:	200–265 lb/90–120 kg (males), 165–230 lb/75–105 kg (females)
Order:	Carpet sharks
Family:	Nurse sharks
Diet:	Fish including rays, squid, octopus, crabs, small invertebrates

Tail fin

An extremely long tail fin makes up about a quarter of the shark's length.

Location

Nurse sharks are found in the tropical (more than 64°F/18°C) waters of the western Atlantic and eastern Pacific Oceans. They swim from the shallows to about 230 feet (70 m) deep.

Coastal	Oceanic
	Sunlit Zone: 0–650 ft (0–200 m)
	Twilight Zone: 650–3,300 ft (200–1,000 m)
	Midnight Zone: 3,300–13,000 ft (1,000–4,000 m)
	Lower Midnight Zone: 13,000–20,000 ft (4,000–6,000 m)

BULL SHARK

The bull shark is a fierce predator that will eat almost anything that it comes across. It is solitary, usually choosing to hunt by itself.

The bull shark is large and has a wide body in relation to its length. It is colored gray on top and off-white below.

It is one of the few sharks that can live in freshwater. Bull sharks are often seen in rivers and lakes. One was spotted 2,485 miles (4,000 km) upstream in the Amazon River in Iquitos, Peru, and they have been known to swim up the Mississippi River as far north as Illinois.

Bull sharks eat all kinds of animals in the water, and this includes other sharks, especially the sandbar shark. They are one of the most dangerous shark species to humans because they are aggressive and often come into shallow coastal waters where people swim and surf. Many of the recorded shark attacks on people have been made by bull sharks.

DISCOVERY FACT™

Bull sharks sometimes use a "bump and bite" technique when on the attack, headbutting their victim first before biting it.

Snout
This is wider than it is long, which is unusual for a shark.

Body
The bull shark has a much wider body in relation to its length than most other sharks.

Profile

Length:	Average 7 ft/2.1 m (males), 11.5 ft/3.5 m (females)
Weight:	200 lb/90 kg (males); 287 lb/130 kg (females)
Order:	Ground sharks
Family:	Requiem sharks
Diet:	Fish (including other sharks), dolphins, turtles, birds, invertebrates

Location

Bull sharks are found worldwide in coastal waters of tropical and subtropical (more than 64°F/18°C) seas and sometimes in rivers. They swim from the surface to about 100 feet (30 m) deep.

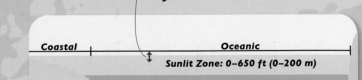

Coastal	Oceanic
	Sunlit Zone: 0–650 ft (0–200 m)
	Twilight Zone: 650–3,300 ft (200–1,000 m)
	Midnight Zone: 3,300–13,000 ft (1,000–4,000 m)
	Lower Midnight Zone: 13,000–20,000 ft (4,000–6,000 m)

TIGER SHARK

Tiger sharks get their name from the stripes and spots that cover the bodies of their young. It also reflects their reputation as large and powerful hunters of the seas.

Tiger sharks are gray-brown on top with a light yellow to white underside. These sharks are some of the largest predatory fish in the seas—the biggest can grow up to 18 feet (5.5 m) long and weigh over 1,760 pounds (800 kg).

Tiger sharks have been called the "garbage cans" of the oceans, since they will eat almost anything. Strange items such as tires, bottles, rolls of chicken wire, and even a crocodile's head have been found in the stomachs of dead tiger sharks.

These sharks are solitary hunters, mostly searching for food at night. They generally swim quite slowly when hunting prey, but they can put on a rapid burst of speed for a vital few seconds when they want to launch an attack.

DISCOVERY FACT™

Scientists in Hawaii found that tiger sharks help protect seagrass meadows by frightening away turtles, who otherwise overgraze the seagrass.

Teeth
Teeth have sharp, jagged edges that can tear and rip virtually anything—even the shells of turtles.

Profile

Length:	Average 10.5 ft/3.2 m (males), 9.5 ft/2.9 m (females)
Weight:	850–1,400 lb/385–635 kg (males and females)
Order:	Ground sharks
Family:	Requiem sharks
Diet:	Fish (including other sharks), turtles, crabs, clams, dolphins, seals, seabirds

Tail fin
The upper part of the tail fin is very long—perfect for swimming quickly as the shark moves in for the kill.

Location
The tiger shark is found worldwide in tropical (more than 64°F/18°C) and some temperate (50–64°F/10–18°C) waters, from the shoreline to the open sea. They swim from the surface to around 1,000 feet (300 m) deep.

Coastal	Oceanic
	Sunlit Zone: 0–650 ft (0–200 m)
	Twilight Zone: 650–3,300 ft (200–1,000 m)
	Midnight Zone: 3,300–13,000 ft (1,000–4,000 m)
	Lower Midnight Zone: 13,000–20,000 ft (4,000–6,000 m)

GREAT WHITE SHARK

The huge and aggressive great white is the most dangerous shark in the world. It has attacked more swimmers, surfers, divers, and small boats than any other species of shark.

A great white shark's body is streamlined and shaped like a torpedo. Despite its name, only its belly is actually white; the top is gray or blue-gray. This is useful when hunting its prey because the great white usually strikes from below—to its prey watching from above, the gray color of its back blends in with the dark water.

The shark's target is normally attacked in a surprise rush and bitten once to stun it. Sometimes, the shark will leap out of the water because of the speed and power of its attack. When the victim is stunned and dying, the shark returns to feed.

The great white is the only shark that pokes its head out of the water. This may be to spot prey such as seals and sea lions swimming on the surface.

DISCOVERY FACT™

The great white shark is the largest predatory fish in the ocean: its bite is about twice as powerful as that of a lion.

Pectoral fins
Large sickle-shaped pectoral fins help the shark to steer through the water.

Profile

Length:	11.5–13 ft/3.5–4 m (males), 15–16.5 ft/4.5–5 m (females), 22 ft/6.7 m maximum
Weight:	Average 1,500–4,000 lb/680–1,815 kg (males and females), 7,000 lb/3,175 kg maximum
Order:	Mackerel sharks
Family:	Mackerel sharks
Diet:	Fish including other sharks, seals, sea lions, dolphins, small whales, sea turtles

Nostrils
An incredible sense of smell can detect one drop of blood in 26 gallons (100 liters) of water and sense blood up to 3 miles (5 km) away.

Teeth
Around 300 huge, triangular, jagged teeth—each one as long as a human finger.

Location
Great white sharks are found worldwide in temperate (50–64°F/10–18°C) waters, and some also are found in tropical (over 64°F/18°C) waters. They swim from the surface to 650 feet (200 m), but have been seen at 3,900 feet (1,200 m).

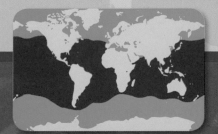

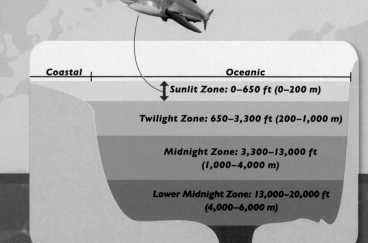

Coastal | Oceanic

Sunlit Zone: 0–650 ft (0–200 m)

Twilight Zone: 650–3,300 ft (200–1,000 m)

Midnight Zone: 3,300–13,000 ft (1,000–4,000 m)

Lower Midnight Zone: 13,000–20,000 ft (4,000–6,000 m)

REEF SHARKS

Sharks are among the most feared animals on the reef. Large reef sharks cruise along the reef edge looking for fish, while smaller sharks hunt shrimps and crabs among the corals.

Blacktip reef shark

The blacktip reef shark is not hunted by any other animals. This shark hunts in shallow water and lagoons. It catches sea snakes as well as fish and octopuses.

Whitetip reef shark

The whitetip reef shark is browny gray in color, but has white tips on its fins. It rests during the day and hunts for food at night in the crevices of the coral reef.

Zebra sharks

Zebra sharks live on the reef. Adults have spots, but when they are young they have stripes, just like a zebra. Their downward-pointing mouth is designed to pick up clams from the seabed. They also hunt crabs and small fish.

A whitetip reef shark rests under a coral ledge.

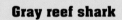

Blacktip reef sharks sometimes bite the legs of people wading in shallow water. Some experts think it is safer to swim through the shallows.

Blacktip reef sharks have distinctive black markings on the ends of their fins.

Gray reef shark

Gray reef sharks are very aggressive fish. If a diver gets too close, the shark will perform a threat display, warning that it is about to attack. It hunches its back and makes a side-to-side movement in the water.

BLACKTIP REEF SHARK

Fast-swimming and active, the blacktip reef shark is one of the three most common sharks inhabiting coral reefs in the tropical waters of the Indian Ocean and the western and central Pacific Ocean. It is mostly found in shallow inshore waters.

These streamlined sharks are brownish-gray on their upper surfaces and white underneath.

They are fast and active hunters, pursuing small fish and invertebrates back and forth around the reef. The patch of water in which they hunt is fairly small in size, and they do not stray far from these home waters, often staying in the same area for years at a time. Most blacktip reef sharks are found near rocky ledges and sandy flats, though they have also been known to swim into brackish (partly salty) water and even into freshwater near the sea.

This shark is fairly timid and does not pose a serious threat to humans. However, it has been known to bite people who came close when swimming, and particularly when wading, in shallow water.

Head
The snout is short and blunt, the eyes are oval, and the mouth is filled with narrow, saw-edged teeth.

Fins
All the fins have black or dark brown tips. This is highlighted on the dorsal fin, which has a light band beneath it.

Profile

Length:	5.2–5.9 ft/1.6–1.8 m (males and females)
Weight:	Up to 31 lb/14 kg (males and females)
Order:	Ground sharks
Family:	Requiem sharks
Diet:	Small fish, squid, shrimps, octopuses (right)

Tail
A sickle-shaped tail fin, built for speed, propels the blacktip reef shark through the water.

Location

Blacktip reef sharks are found in the shallow tropical (more than 64°F/18°C) waters of the Indian and Pacific Oceans and the eastern Mediterranean Sea. They swim from the shallows to about 230 feet (70 m) deep.

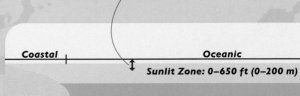

Coastal | Oceanic

Sunlit Zone: 0–650 ft (0–200 m)

Twilight Zone: 650–3,300 ft (200–1,000 m)

Midnight Zone: 3,300–13,000 ft (1,000–4,000 m)

Lower Midnight Zone: 13,000–20,000 ft (4,000–6,000 m)

CARIBBEAN REEF SHARK

The Caribbean reef shark is one of the most common sharks in the Caribbean. It is most active at night when it hunts for fish and invertebrates to eat.

A Caribbean reef shark has the muscular, streamlined shape that is typical of requiem sharks. It has a dark gray to gray-brown back, and white to light yellow stomach.

Caribbean reef sharks live near coral reefs and ocean bottoms near the continental and island shelves. They prefer shallow waters with a maximum depth of 100 feet (30 m). They feed mainly on small fish, which they grasp in the corner of the mouth. They use a sudden sideways snap of the jaws.

These torpedo-shaped sharks have become a major attraction for scuba divers exploring the clear waters of the Caribbean, and some people stage shark feeds for tourists. Critics claim that this changes the natural balance of the food chain—the sharks may start to see humans as reliable sources of food, increasing the chances of a shark attack on humans.

DISCOVERY FACT™

These sharks are often found on the outer edges of coral reefs and sometimes even lying motionless on the ocean floor as if sleeping.

Fins
The tips of the lower fins are dark, as are the rear edges of the large tail fin.

Profile

Length:	6.5–8 ft/2–2.5 m (males), up to 10 ft/3 m (females)
Weight:	Up to 154 lb/70 kg (males and females)
Order:	Ground sharks
Family:	Requiem sharks
Diet:	Fish including rays, invertebrates such as octopuses and squid

Eyes

Large circular eyes, with protective third eyelids that can be drawn across the eyes as protection.

Location

Caribbean reef sharks are found in the shallow tropical (more than 64°F/18°C) waters of the western Atlantic Ocean, as far south as northern Brazil. These streamlined sharks swim from the shallows to about 100 feet (30 m) deep.

Coastal | Oceanic

Sunlit Zone: 0–650 ft (0–200 m)

Twilight Zone: 650–3,300 ft (200–1,000 m)

Midnight Zone: 3,300–13,000 ft (1,000–4,000 m)

Lower Midnight Zone: 13,000–20,000 ft (4,000–6,000 m)

WHITETIP REEF SHARK

One of the most common sharks found around coral reefs in the Indian and Pacific Oceans, the whitetip reef shark is typically found on or near the bottom in clear water.

During the day, whitetip reef sharks spend much of their time resting inside caves or even out in the open, lying on the seabed. Unlike other requiem sharks, which must constantly swim to breathe, the whitetip can lie still on the bottom without fear of drowning, as it can pump water over its gills.

At night, whitetips start to hunt. Their bodies are ideal for wriggling their way into gaps in the reef in pursuit of fish. They sometimes break off pieces of the coral in their eagerness to snatch the prey. Their target fish are beyond the reach of other species of shark that feed in open water. For this reason, whitetips are able to live alongside other species of reef shark without competing for the same sources of food.

Body
The long, thin body is perfect for worming its way into small cracks in the reef.

Head
The head is short but broad, with whiskerlike skin flaps beside the nostrils, called "barbels."

DISCOVERY FACT™

The thick skin of the whitetip reef shark is tough enough to avoid getting cut or grazed when bumping into the sharp coral.

Profile

Length:	3.6–5.2 ft/1–1.6 m (males and females)
Weight:	Up to 40 lb/18 kg (males and females)
Order:	Ground sharks
Family:	Requiem sharks
Diet:	Fish, octopuses, crabs, spiny lobsters (right)

Fins
Prominent white tips on the first dorsal fin and the tail fin give the whitetip reef shark its name.

Location
Whitetip reef sharks are found in the shallow tropical and subtropical (more than 64°F/18°C) waters of the Indian and Pacific Oceans and along the western coast of Central America. They swim from the shallows to about 130 feet (40 m) deep.

Coastal | Oceanic

Sunlit Zone: 0–650 ft (0–200 m)

Twilight Zone: 650–3,300 ft (200–1,000 m)

Midnight Zone: 3,300–13,000 ft (1,000–4,000 m)

Lower Midnight Zone: 13,000–20,000 ft (4,000–6,000 m)

REEF DEFENSE

Reef animals protect themselves from sharks and other predators in different ways. Some use body armor or poisons to defend themselves. Others rely on camouflage to keep them hidden on the reef.

Hiding in coral

Corals make great hiding places for the creatures that live on them. To escape from the many kinds of predator that are trying to eat them, they can hide in the thousands of cracks and crevices that are part of the reef structure.

Body armor

Seahorses use body armor to defend themselves. The tough armor gives them good protection, but makes swimming more difficult. They stay still much of the time, relying on their camouflage to hide them from hungry hunters.

Frog camouflage

Frog fish look more like a piece of coral or sponge than a fish. By keeping perfectly still, they blend in with the reef and are difficult for predators to spot.

Hide and seek

Tiny animals, such as this small goby, hide from their predators on and among the coral branches. The smallest gobies are less than ½ inch (1 cm) long.

Many of the animals that live in the reef are nocturnal: they hide during the day in caves and crevices then come out to feed in the safety of the dark.

Spiny defense

The cowfish's spiky body armor, with long spines over each eye, gives it an unusual appearance. If the cowfish is attacked, it can also release a poison into the water from its skin.

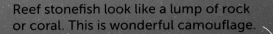

Reef stonefish look like a lump of rock or coral. This is wonderful camouflage.

SURFACE WATERS

The open oceans are home to fewer animals than coastal waters and coral reefs. Most animals that live here are found in the surface layer, which is the top 650 feet (200 m).

DISCOVERY FACT™

During storms at sea, it's not unusual for waves to reach more than 100 feet (30 m) in height: that is as tall as a ten-story building!

Light in the water

The ocean's surface is lit by sunlight. The top 100 feet (30 m) is bright, but it gets darker as you go deeper. By 650 feet (200 m), all light has gone, and the water looks blue-black.

Surface waves

When the wind blows over the surface of the ocean, it creates waves. As the waves grow larger, they are moved along by the wind, and this helps to mix up the water.

Countershading

Many sharks have dark backs and white stomachs. This is called "countershading." From above, their dark backs blend with the depths of the water below. From below, their light stomachs blend with the sunlight coming from above.

The wind blowing over the surface of the sea pushes along wind-powered boats, such as this yacht.

Flying fish

The flying fish has an unusual way of escaping predators. When threatened, it swims straight at the surface of the water and flies into the air, using its fins like wings. It can glide above the surface for up to 330 feet (100 m).

MOVING UP AND DOWN

The plant plankton that form the basis of the ocean food chain live near the surface because they need sunlight for photosynthesis.

During the day, the brightly lit surface waters are virtually empty of small animals. Most dive to the safety of the darker water below. They return to feed under the cover of darkness.

Nighttime travelers

This daily movement is only a few hundred yards, but for tiny animals, such as shrimps and copepods, it is a long journey. It is the only way to feed in safety.

Shrimp

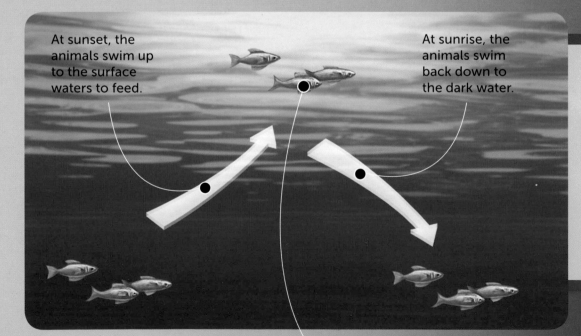

At sunset, the animals swim up to the surface waters to feed.

At sunrise, the animals swim back down to the dark water.

At night, the animals feed on plankton.

Mass migration

Most types of plankton and some types of plankton-eating fish migrate up and down, including krill, herring, and mackerel.

Lantern fish

Lantern fish travel the greatest distances each day. During the day, they are found more than 5,600 feet (1,700 m) down, and at night they rise to within 330 feet (100 m) of the surface. They get their name from the glowing light organs (called "photophores") along their body.

Tiger shark

The tiger shark is one of the largest sharks. It hunts mainly at night when it comes up near the surface of the water. During the day, it goes deeper down into the ocean, usually to around 1,000 feet (300 m).

The tiger shark eats all sorts of marine creatures, including dolphins, seals, turtles, fish, and even other sharks.

WHALE SHARK

This is a true giant—the largest fish in the ocean. Despite its name, it is not a whale, but a gigantic shark that cruises slowly through the sea, sucking in vast amounts of water as it filter feeds.

The whale shark has distinctive light-yellow markings (random stripes and spots) dotted across its skin. Its skin can be up to 4 inches (10 cm) thick. The underlying color is usually dark gray, blue, or brown. Three large ridges run down each side of its body.

These sharks live in warm water, normally out in the open sea, although they do also come fairly close to shore. They are usually solitary feeders, swimming near the surface, where they scoop up vast amounts of plankton and small fish in their huge mouths. These are sieved from the water using a technique called "filter feeding."

Whale sharks have no teeth and are quite harmless to humans. They are not worried by scuba divers coming close to them in the water.

Mouth
A huge gaping mouth vacuums up plankton and small fish.

Profile

Length:	20–40 ft/6–12 m (males and females)
Weight:	Typically around 16.5 tons (males and females), 22.5 tons maximum
Order:	Carpet sharks
Family:	Whale sharks
Diet:	Plankton (right), small fish, crustaceans

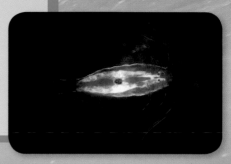

Gill slits

Large bristly gill rakers, behind each gill slit, filter particles of food from the water.

Location

Whale sharks are found worldwide in tropical (more than 64°F/18°C) and warm temperate (50–64°F/10–18°C) waters. They swim from the surface to 2,300 feet (700 m) deep.

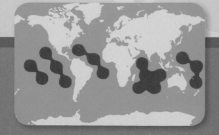

Coastal	Oceanic
	Sunlit Zone: 0–650 ft (0–200 m)
	Twilight Zone: 650–3,300 ft (200–1,000 m)
	Midnight Zone: 3,300–13,000 ft (1,000–4,000 m)
	Lower Midnight Zone: 13,000–20,000 ft (4,000–6,000 m)

BLUE SHARK

The blue shark is a long-distance traveler. It swims hundreds of miles every year, searching for food or to mate.

The blue shark has a bright blue back and a white stomach—these colors help to hide it in the ocean. Viewed from above, the deep blue blends with the murky waters; viewed from below, the white helps the shark to blend in with the light coming from above.

These large sharks hunt with their mouths wide open, trapping small fish, such as sardines, in their jaws. They also feed on squid and other invertebrates, such as octopuses and cuttlefish.

Blue sharks are generally slow swimmers but they can move very quickly when attacking their prey. They travel long distances in their widespread habitat. One blue shark made a trip of 3,740 miles (5,980 km) from New York to the coast of Brazil!

Tail
A long tail provides swimming power as the tail moves from side to side.

Eyes
Large eyes are protected by a transparent third eyelid, which the shark can flick over the eyeball when it is hunting.

Pectoral fins
Long pectoral fins— the same length as the distance between the tip of the snout and the last gill slit.

DISCOVERY FACT™

When migrating across the North Atlantic, female blue sharks appear to ride the strong currents to conserve energy.

Profile

Length:	6–9.3 ft/1.8–2.8 m long (males), 7.2–10.8 ft/2.2–3.3 m long (females)
Weight:	60–120 lb/27–54 kg (males); 205–400 lb/93–181 kg (females)
Order:	Ground sharks
Family:	Requiem sharks
Diet:	Bony fish, squid, and other invertebrates

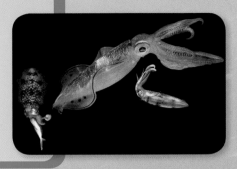

Teeth

Teeth with jagged edges ensure a better grip on squid and other slimy sea creatures with slippery bodies.

Location

Blue sharks are found worldwide in temperate (50–64°F/10–18°C) waters and at lower depths in tropical (more than 64°F/18°C) waters. They swim from the surface to about 1,150 feet (350 m) deep.

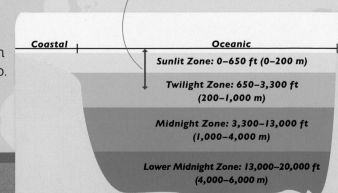

Coastal | Oceanic

Sunlit Zone: 0–650 ft (0–200 m)

Twilight Zone: 650–3,300 ft (200–1,000 m)

Midnight Zone: 3,300–13,000 ft (1,000–4,000 m)

Lower Midnight Zone: 13,000–20,000 ft (4,000–6,000 m)

GREAT HAMMERHEAD SHARK

There are nine species of hammerhead sharks, and the great hammerhead is the biggest of them. The shape of their head is unique.

Great hammerhead sharks are gray-brown to olive green on top, with an off-white underside.

No one knows for sure why their head has such a strange shape. Scientists think that the extra distance between the eyes gives the shark a huge field of vision both above and below. Masses of special sensors on the underside of the "hammer" may allow it to detect the presence of stingrays when they are lying buried in the sand on the sea floor. Some hammerheads have even been seen to pin a stingray to the sea floor with their heads while they take a bite out of its wings to stop it escaping.

Great hammerheads migrate—they head to warmer waters during the winter and then return to their normal feeding grounds in summer.

Dorsal fin
A tall and pointed dorsal fin helps to stabilize the shark when it is turning quickly in the water as it hunts for prey.

Head
The head is shaped like a flattened hammer with the eyes set at the edges.

Tail

A tall tail fin made up of a large upper section, called a lobe, and a smaller lower section, propels the shark through the water.

Profile

Length:	13–20 ft/4–6 m (males and females)
Weight:	500–1,000 lb/227–454 kg (males and females)
Order:	Ground sharks
Family:	Hammerhead sharks
Diet:	Fish, including rays (below) and other sharks, squid, octopuses, crustaceans

Location

Great hammerheads are found worldwide in tropical and subtropical (more than 64°F/18°C) waters. They swim from the surface to about 260 feet (80 m) deep.

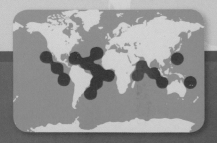

Coastal	Oceanic
	Sunlit Zone: 0–650 ft (0–200 m)
	Twilight Zone: 650–3,300 ft (200–1,000 m)
	Midnight Zone: 3,300–13,000 ft (1,000–4,000 m)
	Lower Midnight Zone: 13,000–20,000 ft (4,000–6,000 m)

SHORTFIN MAKO SHARK

This is one of the fastest sharks in the ocean. It can reach a speed of up to 30 miles per hour (48 km/h) when chasing after prey and can leap clear out of the water to heights of up to 20 feet (6 m) above the surface.

The shortfin mako shark's upper side is metallic blue while the underside is white. This countershading makes the shark hard to spot in the water when seen both from above and from below.

The shortfin mako's speed allows it to feed on quick-moving fish, such as tuna, swordfish, and even other sharks. It is able to hunt them because it swims faster than they do.

Due to their size and speed, shortfin makos can be dangerous to humans. There have been a number of attacks on swimmers and divers, and some of them have been fatal. Divers have reported that the shark will swim in a figure-of-eight pattern before launching an attack with its mouth open.

DISCOVERY FACT™

Shortfin mako sharks prey on swordfish, but their victims sometimes fight back and may even manage to kill the sharks with their "swords."

Body shape
Sleek and streamlined with a long, cone-shaped snout. It slips easily through the water, which helps the shark to swim so fast.

Profile

Length:	Average 6–8 ft/1.8–2-4 m (males and females), 12.8 ft/3.9 m maximum
Weight:	Average 132–300 lb/60–136 kg (males and females), 1,250 lb (567 kg) maximum
Order:	Mackerel sharks
Family:	Mackerel sharks
Diet:	Fish, including other sharks, rays, squid, dolphins (right), small whales

Teeth
Slender, slightly curved, and pointed teeth, with razor-sharp edges, help the mako grip slippery, fast-moving fish.

Location
Shortfin mako sharks are found worldwide in warm temperate (50–64°F/10–18°C) and tropical (over 64°F/18°C) waters. They swim from the surface to around 500 feet (150 m).

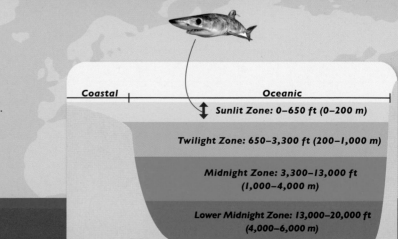

Coastal   Oceanic

Sunlit Zone: 0–650 ft (0–200 m)

Twilight Zone: 650–3,300 ft (200–1,000 m)

Midnight Zone: 3,300–13,000 ft (1,000–4,000 m)

Lower Midnight Zone: 13,000–20,000 ft (4,000–6,000 m)

SILKY SHARK

This is one of the most common sharks in the open ocean. There are tens of millions of these slim, agile predators living in tropical waters around the world.

The back of the silky shark ranges in color from dark brown to blue-gray. The underside is generally white, and the lower fins can have dark tips on their underside.

This shark usually hunts on its own, and generally attacks fish that are swimming in open water. It is particularly attracted to tuna and is often seen trailing behind shoals of these fish. Sometimes, when there are lots of fish in the water, silky sharks will hunt together in a pack. They "herd" the shoal toward the surface. Then they slice into the shoal with their mouths open, to trap them in their jaws.

Silky sharks can act aggressively toward humans, but because they are normally found out in the open ocean, they do not often come into contact with divers.

Skin
The skin is smooth to the touch, unlike the skin of other species of sharks, which is rough.

Pectoral fin
Long, curved pectoral fins give the shark lift as it swims through the water.

Dorsal fin
A short, rounded dorsal fin helps the silky shark balance.

Profile

Length:	6–7 ft/1.8–2.1 m (males), 7–7.5 ft/2.1–2.3 m (females)
Weight:	385–660 lb/175–300 kg (males and females), 800 lb (363 kg) maximum
Order:	Ground sharks
Family:	Requiem sharks
Diet:	Fish (right), squid, crustaceans

Location
Silky sharks are found worldwide in tropical and subtropical waters, usually at a temperature of 73°F (23°C) or more. They swim from around 60 feet (18 m) to about 1,640 feet (500 m) deep.

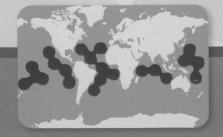

Coastal	Oceanic
	Sunlit Zone: 0–650 ft (0–200 m)
	Twilight Zone: 650–3,300 ft (200–1,000 m)
	Midnight Zone: 3,300–13,000 ft (1,000–4,000 m)
	Lower Midnight Zone: 13,000–20,000 ft (4,000–6,000 m)

OCEANIC WHITETIP SHARK

Oceanic whitetip sharks live in the open ocean. They often follow ships hoping to pick up scraps of food thrown overboard. For this reason, sailors used to call them "sea dogs."

The upper surface of the oceanic whitetip shark's body varies from grayish-bronze to brown in color, depending upon where it is in the world. The underside is whitish, sometimes with a yellow tinge.

The oceanic whitetip usually hunts alone, although groups may form when individuals converge on food. It tends to cruise in the open ocean near to the surface. It covers vast stretches of empty water scanning for food by day and night, and is quite slow-moving. However, when it gets near its prey—usually fish or invertebrates—it can put on sudden bursts of speed.

Although they are not usually found near shore, oceanic whitetips are dangerous to humans because of their predatory nature. During World War II, they caused the deaths of many sailors and airmen who found themselves in the water after their ships were sunk or their aircraft were shot down.

DISCOVERY FACT™

When an oceanic whitetip senses the smell of blood, it may go into a "feeding frenzy," swimming around wildly and biting anything that comes near.

Teeth
Sharp triangular upper teeth and smaller pointed lower teeth are ideal for holding and tearing the shark's prey.

Dorsal fins
This shark has a big, rounded first fin on its back.

Profile

Length:	Up to 10 ft/3 m (males and females)
Weight:	77–154 lb/35–70 kg (males and females), 368 lb/167 kg maximum
Order:	Ground sharks
Family:	Requiem sharks
Diet:	Fish, squid and other mollusks, sea turtles, crustaceans

Pectoral fins
Long, paddlelike fins are set low behind the gill slits. All the large fins have white tips.

Location
Oceanic whitetip sharks are found worldwide in tropical waters, usually at temperatures between 68 and 82°F (20–28°C). They swim from the surface to about 500 feet (150 m) deep.

Coastal	Oceanic
	Sunlit Zone: 0–650 ft (0–200 m)
	Twilight Zone: 650–3,300 ft (200–1,000 m)
	Midnight Zone: 3,300–13,000 ft (1,000–4,000 m)
	Lower Midnight Zone: 13,000–20,000 ft (4,000–6,000 m)

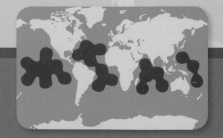

GOING DOWN

As you descend, the sea becomes darker and colder. The pressure increases, too. In very deep water, a diver would be crushed and all the air squeezed from their lungs. Only animals adapted to this environment can survive. The surface layer goes down to about 650 feet (200 m). Next comes the twilight zone, down to 3,300 feet (1,000 m). The midnight zone stretches to the seabed.

DISCOVERY FACT™

The frilled shark lives in deep waters in the twilight zone. It is shaped like an eel, with a huge mouth containing around 300 needlelike teeth.

Sunlit zone

Sunlight passes through the water to a depth of about 650 feet (200 m).

Here in the surface layer, there is enough light for plant plankton and seaweeds to make their food.

Nurse sharks spend most of their time in the sunny surface layer of the sea.

Sixgill sharks are found down near the deep seabed.

Twilight zone

Beneath the surface layer, there is a glimmer of light—just enough for some animals to see. Animals dive down from the surface into this layer for safety.

Midnight zone

The midnight zone is pitch black and cold, and the water is still. Fish and other sea creatures living below 1,640 feet (500 m) are designed to withstand the great pressure of the surrounding water.

Sperm whales can stay underwater for well over an hour without taking a breath, and can dive to incredible depths.

Coastal	Oceanic
	Sunlit Zone: 0–650 ft (0–200 m)
	Twilight Zone: 650–3,300 ft (200–1,000 m)
	Midnight Zone: 3,300–13,000 ft (1,000–4,000 m)
	Lower Midnight Zone: 13,000–20,000 ft (4,000–6,000 m)

GOBLIN SHARK

Very little is known about the goblin shark as it lives in the deep ocean. Only about 45 specimens have been studied to date.

Goblin sharks are not often seen because they live in deep water at the bottom of the ocean. They are only seen when they are caught in the fishing nets of deep-sea trawlers. The goblin shark is pink-gray in color because its blood vessels lie close to the surface of the skin and can be seen through it.

It is very dark in the deep ocean, so the goblin shark does not rely on its eyesight to detect prey. Scientists think that special organs on its long snout can detect the faint electrical fields created by other fish and invertebrates when they move. It may also use its snout to dig up fish and crustaceans that are hiding in the sand and silt on the seafloor.

A goblin shark's jaws act like a spring-loaded trap. The teeth and jaws can be catapulted forward, a little like opening a telescope, to snatch a fish from the water. Then they spring back to their normal position.

Body
The body is soft and quite rubbery. The caudal fin is very long compared to the two dorsal fins.

Length:	10–13 ft/3–4 m (males and females)
Weight:	Around 400 lb/181 kg (males and females), 463 lb (210 kg) maximum
Order:	Mackerel sharks
Family:	Goblin sharks
Diet:	Fish, squid (right) and other mollusks, crustaceans

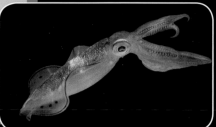

Snout
The large flattened snout protrudes from the top of its head. Beneath this are the jaws with slender, fanglike teeth.

Location
Goblin sharks have been found off the coasts of Japan, Australia, New Zealand, and southern Africa, and in the eastern Atlantic and Indian Oceans. They swim near the bottom about 820 feet (250 m) deep, but they can go down to 3,950 feet (1,200 m) or more.

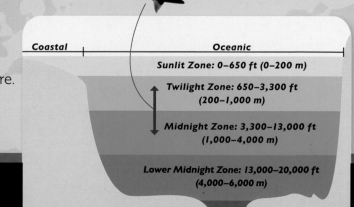

Coastal | Oceanic

Sunlit Zone: 0–650 ft (0–200 m)

Twilight Zone: 650–3,300 ft (200–1,000 m)

Midnight Zone: 3,300–13,000 ft (1,000–4,000 m)

Lower Midnight Zone: 13,000–20,000 ft (4,000–6,000 m)

SIXGILL SHARK

This big shark normally lives in the darkness of deep oceans at around 6,560 feet (2,000 m).

The sixgill shark ranges in color from gray and olive green to brown on the upper side, fading to a paler underside. There is a light-colored stripe along each flank. It has small, teardrop-shaped, green eyes with black pupils.

It normally hunts on its own, swimming slowly and steadily through the water searching for food. When it spots something to eat, it accelerates rapidly to catch its prey. The teeth in its lower jaw are shaped like the blade of a saw. The shark uses them to rip the flesh off the body of large fish that it cannot swallow whole.

Sixgill sharks are not considered dangerous to humans because they are quite shy and not aggressive unless provoked. Also, they generally keep to deep waters where divers cannot follow them.

Gills
Most sharks have five gill slits on each side of their bodies, but the sixgill shark has six long slits.

DISCOVERY FACT™

The sixgill shark rests in the deep ocean during the day, but swims up to the surface at night to hunt for fish and seals.

Dorsal fin
There is only one dorsal fin on this shark's back, set quite a long way back toward the tail.

Location

Sixgill sharks are found worldwide in tropical (over 64°F/18°C) and temperate (50–64°F/10–18°C) waters. They usually swim from about 295 feet (90 m) to as deep as 6,560 feet (2,000 m).

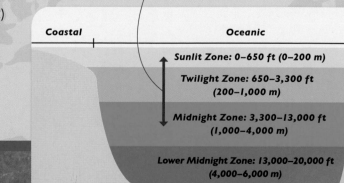

Coastal | Oceanic

Sunlit Zone: 0–650 ft (0–200 m)

Twilight Zone: 650–3,300 ft (200–1,000 m)

Midnight Zone: 3,300–13,000 ft (1,000–4,000 m)

Lower Midnight Zone: 13,000–20,000 ft (4,000–6,000 m)

GETTING CLOSE TO SHARKS

Many people are curious about sharks—they are big, powerful, and fascinating animals. There are different ways that we can see them up close.

DISCOVERY FACT™

Scientists can now study dangerous species using radio-controlled unmanned submarines that are able to locate, track, and film the animals at close quarters.

Diving with sharks

In the clear, warm waters of the tropics, diving with sharks has become a tourist attraction. Some dive companies even organize shark feeds to attract sharks to a particular spot.

In the aquarium

One way that people can get close to sharks is to visit one of the many aquariums that display them to the public. As well as providing a tourist attraction, these sea-life centers allow scientists to study shark behavior in order to help protect them.

Shark cages

The great white shark is seen as the ultimate man-eater. It is now possible for tourists to watch great whites from inside the safety of a submerged metal cage.

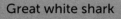 Great white shark

On the screen

Television has had a huge impact on our knowledge of sharks. Nature programs give us an insight into their behavior and habits. Movies such as *Jaws* and *Deep Blue Sea* portray the shark as a deadly monster.

Divers can take photographs of huge sharks while safe inside the cage.

SHARK ATTACKS

Whenever a shark attacks someone swimming offshore, it makes news all around the world, particularly if the victim is killed. But most experts agree that the risk of being attacked by a shark is very small.

Attacks are rare

Worldwide, there are only around 70 to 100 attacks in an average year, of which around 10 to 15 are fatal. More people are killed by bees each year than by sharks.

Surfing star

In October 2003, 13-year-old Bethany Hamilton was surfing off the coast of Hawaii when she was attacked by a tiger shark. It bit off her left arm. She survived the attack and returned to the water 26 days later. In 2007, she became a professional surfer.

When sharks attack surfers, they probably mistake the outline of the surfboard for prey.

Survivor

One of the world's leading authorities on the great white shark, Rodney Fox, was himself the victim of a terrible attack in 1963. He was almost bitten in half and his wounds needed more than 450 stitches. Since then, he has dedicated his life to the appreciation and preservation of the great white shark.

A fighting chance

Anyone who is unlucky enough to be attacked by a shark should try to fight back by hitting the shark on its snout and clawing at its eyes and gills.

The eyes and snout are a shark's vulnerable areas.

OCEANS IN DANGER

The oceans are important to people. We transport essential goods on them by ship and get food and natural resources from the sea. However, we also damage the oceans through pollution and overfishing, and this creates problems for sharks.

Sharks sometimes become tangled in nets and die.

Dangers of pollution

When there is an oil spill or when waste materials are dumped at sea, humans are contributing to the pollution of the oceans. Pollution can contaminate fish that come into contact with it. When sharks eat contaminated fish, they end up with high levels of dangerous chemicals in their bodies.

Accidents at sea often lead to ocean pollution.

Polluting sewage

Millions of gallons of sewage are emptied into the oceans each year by people. Fish that live in coastal waters can be harmed by sewage. This also harms sharks that feed on the fish living in these waters.

Garbage dumped at sea

Waste material thrown into the sea includes discarded fishing lines, nets, and plastics in which sharks sometimes get entangled. If they cannot get free, they will die in the water.

Not many young

Sharks are slow to mature and may produce just a few young in any breeding cycle. This means that when populations are hit by overfishing or ocean pollution, the numbers take a very long time to recover.

SHARK FISHING

Many sharks are known as apex predators. This means that they kill and eat other animals, but that virtually no predators in the oceans kill them. However, sharks do have one deadly enemy that lives on land—humans.

Commercial fishing

Every year, around 100 million sharks are caught and killed. This is because a lot of people earn their living by catching sharks. Shark products, including meat, the fins, the skin, and the teeth, are sold in huge quantities.

Unwanted victims

Sharks are often caught in trawler nets or on longline hooks that have been set to catch other fish, such as tuna or swordfish. The sharks die, even though the fisherman do not want them. They are known as "by-catch."

Sport fishing

In certain parts of the world, the sport of fishing for big game fish is very popular. Some fishermen release the fish after it has been caught and photographed, but others kill their catch to keep as a trophy.

Sharks are one of the game fish that sport fisherman try to catch using fast boats like this.

Shark's fin soup

A thick soup made from shark fins is very popular in the Far East. It is thought to have medicinal properties. Some fishermen catch sharks, cut off their fins, and then throw the sharks back in the water. Millions die in this way.

PROTECTING SHARKS

Although changes in the world's weather, the effects of pollution, and the impact of fishing all spell danger for sharks, many people are trying to protect and conserve shark populations around the globe.

Shark sanctuaries

Some countries have banned commercial fishing in their national waters (the parts of the sea that they control), to help protect sharks. The island groups of Palau, in the western Pacific Ocean, and the Maldives, in the Indian Ocean, have both done this.

Palau, a country made up of around 250 Pacific islands, has created a protected area for sharks.

How can we help?

We can help sharks survive in the wild by not buying shark products, which encourages shark fishing. We can also try to persuade politicians to change the laws that govern how commercial fishing is done. Some people are trying to get laws changed so that sharks are better protected.

Acting responsibly

Tourists who want to see and swim with sharks should make sure that the dive company treats sharks with proper care.

Better understanding
Scientific research, sea-life visitor centers, television programs, magazine articles, movies, and books all help the general public to understand that sharks are remarkable creatures.

Scientists tag a shortfin mako shark, to help track its migrations.

DISCOVERY FACT™

A shortfin mako shark tagged by scientists in New Zealand and tracked by satellite traveled more than 8,260 miles (13,290 km) in seven months.

Aquariums are great places to learn about sharks and see them close up.

GLOSSARY

Barbels
Whiskerlike feelers near the nostrils and mouth of some sharks. They are used to taste and feel.

Camouflage
A special coloring or body shape that blends with the surroundings, so that an animal is not easily seen by predators or prey.

Carnivore
An animal that eats other animals.

Cartilage
Tough, light, and stretchy material from which a shark's skeleton is made.

Copepod
A tiny, shrimplike crustacean that lives in the water.

Countershading
A form of camouflage found in many sharks and other fish, in which the skin of the back is dark and the underside light.

Crustacean
An invertebrate animal that has an outer shell (an exoskeleton) and jointed legs, such as lobsters, crabs, and shrimps.

Dorsal fin
The tall fin that stands upright on a shark's back.

Gill
The parts of the body used by fish and some other animals to breathe underwater.

Gill rakers
Sievelike structures that divert solid materials away from the gills.

Habitat
The name given to the place where an animal or plant lives.

Invertebrate
An animal that does not have a backbone.

Lagoon
An area of salty water cut off from the sea by a bank of shingle, sand, or coral.

Larva
The growing stage of an animal such as a young fish or squid.

Lateral line
A row of sense organs along the side of fish, used to detect movement and vibrations in the surrounding water.

Mammal
A warm-blooded animal. Female mammals give birth to live young and feed them with their own milk.

Marine
To do with the sea.

Migration
A regular journey made by an animal, sometimes over very long distances.

Mollusk
An animal with a soft body, usually protected by an outer shell.

Nocturnal
Being active at night rather than during the day.

Nutrient
A substance that is needed for healthy growth and living.

Organism
A living thing such as an animal, plant, fungus, or bacterium.

Pectoral fins
The fins that stick out of the sides of a shark's body.

Photosynthesis
The process by which plants use sunlight and the green chlorophyll in their leaves to make sugars that give the plant energy.

Phytoplankton
Tiny plants that float freely in the ocean currents.

Plankton
The tiny plants and animals that are found floating close to the surface of ponds, lakes, and seas. They are the basis of the marine food chain.

Polar
To do with the areas around the North and South Poles.

Pollution
The act of making something, such as the air or the water, unclean by discharging harmful substances into it.

Population
The number of individuals living in a particular area.

Predator
An animal that hunts and feeds on other animals.

Prey
An animal that is hunted by other animals.

Pupil
The central part of an eye that lets in light.

Respiratory system
The parts of a body that allow an organism to breathe.

Sensor
Part of an organism that responds to a particular

stimulus, such as light, sound, or heat.

Shoal
A group of fish, often of the same species, that swim together for protection. Also known as a "school."

Solitary
A plant or animal that lives alone.

Sonar
A way of finding the position of objects or prey by using sound waves that travel through the water.

Streamlined
Having a shape that slips easily through air or a liquid, like a torpedo, for instance.

Structure
The way something is built or put together.

Subtropical
Relating to the areas of Earth next to the tropical zone, with a more temperate climate.

Swim bladder
A gas-filled organ inside a fish that stops it from sinking in the water.

Tropical
Relating to a part of the Earth that lies close to the Equator. The climate in the tropical zone is hot and wet for most of the year.

Vertebrate
An animal that has a backbone.

Yolk
The sac of protein in the egg that nourishes the developing embryo.

Zooplankton
Tiny animals that float freely in the ocean currents.

INDEX